WITH THIS

RING

EVERYTHING

MARRIAGE

I0492403

Happy is the man who finds a true friend, and far happier is
he who finds that true friend in his wife -Franz Schubert-

Happy is the man who finds a true friend, and far happier is
he who finds that true friend in his wife -Franz Schubert-

Happy is the man who finds a true friend, and far happier is he who finds that true friend in his wife -Franz Schubert-

Happy is the man who finds a true friend, and far happier is
he who finds that true friend in his wife -Franz Schubert-

Happy is the man who finds a true friend, and far happier is
he who finds that true friend in his wife -Franz Schubert-

Happy is the man who finds a true friend, and far happier is
he who finds that true friend in his wife -Franz Schubert-

Happy is the man who finds a true friend, and far happier is he who finds that true friend in his wife -Franz Schubert-

Happy is the man who finds a true friend, and far happier is he who finds that true friend in his wife -Franz Schubert-

Happy is the man who finds a true friend, and far happier is he who finds that true friend in his wife -Franz Schubert-

Happy is the man who finds a true friend, and far happier is
he who finds that true friend in his wife -Franz Schubert-

Happy is the man who finds a true friend, and far happier is he who finds that true friend in his wife -Franz Schubert-

Happy is the man who finds a true friend, and far happier is
he who finds that true friend in his wife -Franz Schubert-

Happy is the man who finds a true friend, and far happier is
he who finds that true friend in his wife -Franz Schubert-

Happy is the man who finds a true friend, and far happier is
he who finds that true friend in his wife -Franz Schubert-

Happy is the man who finds a true friend, and far happier is
he who finds that true friend in his wife -Franz Schubert-

Happy is the man who finds a true friend, and far happier is he who finds that true friend in his wife -Franz Schubert-

Happy is the man who finds a true friend, and far happier is he who finds that true friend in his wife -Franz Schubert-

Happy is the man who finds a true friend, and far happier is he who finds that true friend in his wife -Franz Schubert-

Happy is the man who finds a true friend, and far happier is
he who finds that true friend in his wife -Franz Schubert-

Happy is the man who finds a true friend, and far happier is
he who finds that true friend in his wife -Franz Schubert-

Happy is the man who finds a true friend, and far happier is
he who finds that true friend in his wife -Franz Schubert-

Happy is the man who finds a true friend, and far happier is
he who finds that true friend in his wife -Franz Schubert-

Happy is the man who finds a true friend, and far happier is he who finds that true friend in his wife -Franz Schubert-

Happy is the man who finds a true friend, and far happier is
he who finds that true friend in his wife -Franz Schubert-

Happy is the man who finds a true friend, and far happier is
he who finds that true friend in his wife -Franz Schubert-

Happy is the man who finds a true friend, and far happier is
he who finds that true friend in his wife -Franz Schubert-

Happy is the man who finds a true friend, and far happier is he who finds that true friend in his wife -Franz Schubert-

Happy is the man who finds a true friend, and far happier is he who finds that true friend in his wife -Franz Schubert-

Happy is the man who finds a true friend, and far happier is
he who finds that true friend in his wife -Franz Schubert-

Happy is the man who finds a true friend, and far happier is
he who finds that true friend in his wife -Franz Schubert-

Happy is the man who finds a true friend, and far happier is he who finds that true friend in his wife -Franz Schubert-

Happy is the man who finds a true friend, and far happier is
he who finds that true friend in his wife -Franz Schubert-

Happy is the man who finds a true friend, and far happier is
he who finds that true friend in his wife -Franz Schubert-

Happy is the man who finds a true friend, and far happier is he who finds that true friend in his wife -Franz Schubert-

Happy is the man who finds a true friend, and far happier is
he who finds that true friend in his wife -Franz Schubert-

Happy is the man who finds a true friend, and far happier is he who finds that true friend in his wife -Franz Schubert-

Happy is the man who finds a true friend, and far happier is he who finds that true friend in his wife -Franz Schubert-

Happy is the man who finds a true friend, and far happier is
he who finds that true friend in his wife -Franz Schubert-

Happy is the man who finds a true friend, and far happier is
he who finds that true friend in his wife -Franz Schubert-

Happy is the man who finds a true friend, and far happier is
he who finds that true friend in his wife -Franz Schubert-

Happy is the man who finds a true friend, and far happier is
he who finds that true friend in his wife -Franz Schubert-

Happy is the man who finds a true friend, and far happier is
he who finds that true friend in his wife -Franz Schubert-

Happy is the man who finds a true friend, and far happier is
he who finds that true friend in his wife -Franz Schubert-

Happy is the man who finds a true friend, and far happier is
he who finds that true friend in his wife -Franz Schubert-

Happy is the man who finds a true friend, and far happier is
he who finds that true friend in his wife -Franz Schubert-

Happy is the man who finds a true friend, and far happier is
he who finds that true friend in his wife -Franz Schubert-

Happy is the man who finds a true friend, and far happier is
he who finds that true friend in his wife -Franz Schubert-

Happy is the man who finds a true friend, and far happier is he who finds that true friend in his wife -Franz Schubert-

Happy is the man who finds a true friend, and far happier is
he who finds that true friend in his wife -Franz Schubert-

Happy is the man who finds a true friend, and far happier is
he who finds that true friend in his wife -Franz Schubert-

Happy is the man who finds a true friend, and far happier is
he who finds that true friend in his wife -Franz Schubert-

Happy is the man who finds a true friend, and far happier is he who finds that true friend in his wife -Franz Schubert-

Happy is the man who finds a true friend, and far happier is
he who finds that true friend in his wife -Franz Schubert-

Happy is the man who finds a true friend, and far happier is
he who finds that true friend in his wife -Franz Schubert-

Happy is the man who finds a true friend, and far happier is
he who finds that true friend in his wife -Franz Schubert-

Happy is the man who finds a true friend, and far happier is
he who finds that true friend in his wife -Franz Schubert-

Happy is the man who finds a true friend, and far happier is
he who finds that true friend in his wife -Franz Schubert-

Happy is the man who finds a true friend, and far happier is
he who finds that true friend in his wife -Franz Schubert-

Happy is the man who finds a true friend, and far happier is
he who finds that true friend in his wife -Franz Schubert-

Happy is the man who finds a true friend, and far happier is he who finds that true friend in his wife -Franz Schubert-

Happy is the man who finds a true friend, and far happier is he who finds that true friend in his wife -Franz Schubert-

Happy is the man who finds a true friend, and far happier is
he who finds that true friend in his wife -Franz Schubert-

Happy is the man who finds a true friend, and far happier is
he who finds that true friend in his wife -Franz Schubert-

Happy is the man who finds a true friend, and far happier is
he who finds that true friend in his wife -Franz Schubert-

Happy is the man who finds a true friend, and far happier is
he who finds that true friend in his wife -Franz Schubert-

Happy is the man who finds a true friend, and far happier is
he who finds that true friend in his wife -Franz Schubert-

Happy is the man who finds a true friend, and far happier is he who finds that true friend in his wife -Franz Schubert-

Happy is the man who finds a true friend, and far happier is
he who finds that true friend in his wife -Franz Schubert-

Happy is the man who finds a true friend, and far happier is
he who finds that true friend in his wife -Franz Schubert-

Happy is the man who finds a true friend, and far happier is
he who finds that true friend in his wife -Franz Schubert-

Happy is the man who finds a true friend, and far happier is
he who finds that true friend in his wife -Franz Schubert-

Happy is the man who finds a true friend, and far happier is
he who finds that true friend in his wife -Franz Schubert-

Happy is the man who finds a true friend, and far happier is
he who finds that true friend in his wife -Franz Schubert-

Happy is the man who finds a true friend, and far happier is
he who finds that true friend in his wife -Franz Schubert-

Happy is the man who finds a true friend, and far happier is
he who finds that true friend in his wife -Franz Schubert-

Happy is the man who finds a true friend, and far happier is
he who finds that true friend in his wife -Franz Schubert-

Happy is the man who finds a true friend, and far happier is he who finds that true friend in his wife -Franz Schubert-

Happy is the man who finds a true friend, and far happier is
he who finds that true friend in his wife -Franz Schubert-

Happy is the man who finds a true friend, and far happier is
he who finds that true friend in his wife -Franz Schubert-

Happy is the man who finds a true friend, and far happier is he who finds that true friend in his wife -Franz Schubert-

Happy is the man who finds a true friend, and far happier is
he who finds that true friend in his wife -Franz Schubert-

Happy is the man who finds a true friend, and far happier is
he who finds that true friend in his wife -Franz Schubert-

Happy is the man who finds a true friend, and far happier is
he who finds that true friend in his wife -Franz Schubert-

Happy is the man who finds a true friend, and far happier is he who finds that true friend in his wife -Franz Schubert-

Happy is the man who finds a true friend, and far happier is
he who finds that true friend in his wife -Franz Schubert-

Happy is the man who finds a true friend, and far happier is he who finds that true friend in his wife -Franz Schubert-

Happy is the man who finds a true friend, and far happier is
he who finds that true friend in his wife -Franz Schubert-

Happy is the man who finds a true friend, and far happier is
he who finds that true friend in his wife -Franz Schubert-

Happy is the man who finds a true friend, and far happier is he who finds that true friend in his wife -Franz Schubert-

Happy is the man who finds a true friend, and far happier is he who finds that true friend in his wife -Franz Schubert-

Happy is the man who finds a true friend, and far happier is
he who finds that true friend in his wife -Franz Schubert-

Happy is the man who finds a true friend, and far happier is
he who finds that true friend in his wife -Franz Schubert-

Happy is the man who finds a true friend, and far happier is
he who finds that true friend in his wife -Franz Schubert-

Happy is the man who finds a true friend, and far happier is
he who finds that true friend in his wife -Franz Schubert-

Happy is the man who finds a true friend, and far happier is he who finds that true friend in his wife -Franz Schubert-

Happy is the man who finds a true friend, and far happier is he who finds that true friend in his wife -Franz Schubert-

Happy is the man who finds a true friend, and far happier is
he who finds that true friend in his wife -Franz Schubert-

Happy is the man who finds a true friend, and far happier is
he who finds that true friend in his wife -Franz Schubert-

Happy is the man who finds a true friend, and far happier is
he who finds that true friend in his wife -Franz Schubert-

Happy is the man who finds a true friend, and far happier is he who finds that true friend in his wife -Franz Schubert-

Happy is the man who finds a true friend, and far happier is
he who finds that true friend in his wife -Franz Schubert-

Happy is the man who finds a true friend, and far happier is
he who finds that true friend in his wife -Franz Schubert-

Happy is the man who finds a true friend, and far happier is
he who finds that true friend in his wife -Franz Schubert-

Happy is the man who finds a true friend, and far happier is he who finds that true friend in his wife -Franz Schubert-

Happy is the man who finds a true friend, and far happier is
he who finds that true friend in his wife -Franz Schubert-

Happy is the man who finds a true friend, and far happier is
he who finds that true friend in his wife -Franz Schubert-

Happy is the man who finds a true friend, and far happier is
he who finds that true friend in his wife -Franz Schubert-

Happy is the man who finds a true friend, and far happier is
he who finds that true friend in his wife -Franz Schubert-

Happy is the man who finds a true friend, and far happier is
he who finds that true friend in his wife -Franz Schubert-

Happy is the man who finds a true friend, and far happier is
he who finds that true friend in his wife -Franz Schubert-

Happy is the man who finds a true friend, and far happier is
he who finds that true friend in his wife -Franz Schubert-

Happy is the man who finds a true friend, and far happier is
he who finds that true friend in his wife -Franz Schubert-

Happy is the man who finds a true friend, and far happier is
he who finds that true friend in his wife -Franz Schubert-

Happy is the man who finds a true friend, and far happier is
he who finds that true friend in his wife -Franz Schubert-

Happy is the man who finds a true friend, and far happier is
he who finds that true friend in his wife -Franz Schubert-

Happy is the man who finds a true friend, and far happier is
he who finds that true friend in his wife -Franz Schubert-

Happy is the man who finds a true friend, and far happier is
he who finds that true friend in his wife -Franz Schubert-

Happy is the man who finds a true friend, and far happier is he who finds that true friend in his wife -Franz Schubert-

130

Happy is the man who finds a true friend, and far happier is
he who finds that true friend in his wife -Franz Schubert-

Happy is the man who finds a true friend, and far happier is
he who finds that true friend in his wife -Franz Schubert-

Happy is the man who finds a true friend, and far happier is
he who finds that true friend in his wife -Franz Schubert-

Happy is the man who finds a true friend, and far happier is
he who finds that true friend in his wife -Franz Schubert-

Happy is the man who finds a true friend, and far happier is
he who finds that true friend in his wife -Franz Schubert-

Happy is the man who finds a true friend, and far happier is
he who finds that true friend in his wife -Franz Schubert-

Happy is the man who finds a true friend, and far happier is
he who finds that true friend in his wife -Franz Schubert-

Happy is the man who finds a true friend, and far happier is he who finds that true friend in his wife -Franz Schubert-

Happy is the man who finds a true friend, and far happier is
he who finds that true friend in his wife -Franz Schubert-

Happy is the man who finds a true friend, and far happier is
he who finds that true friend in his wife -Franz Schubert-

Happy is the man who finds a true friend, and far happier is
he who finds that true friend in his wife -Franz Schubert-

Happy is the man who finds a true friend, and far happier is he who finds that true friend in his wife -Franz Schubert-

Happy is the man who finds a true friend, and far happier is he who finds that true friend in his wife -Franz Schubert-

Happy is the man who finds a true friend, and far happier is
he who finds that true friend in his wife -Franz Schubert-

Happy is the man who finds a true friend, and far happier is
he who finds that true friend in his wife -Franz Schubert-

Happy is the man who finds a true friend, and far happier is
he who finds that true friend in his wife -Franz Schubert-

Happy is the man who finds a true friend, and far happier is
he who finds that true friend in his wife -Franz Schubert-

Happy is the man who finds a true friend, and far happier is he who finds that true friend in his wife -Franz Schubert-

HAPPY WIFE
HAPPY LIFE

www.ingramcontent.com/pod-product-compliance
Lightning Source LLC
Chambersburg PA
CBHW071312220526
45468CB00001B/343